PERSONAL EFFECTS
NEW AND SELECTED POEMS

BY
DANIEL J. LANGTON

BLUE LIGHT PRESS ◆ 1ST WORLD PUBLISHING

SAN FRANCISCO ◆ FAIRFIELD ◆ DELHI

PERSONAL EFFECTS

Copyright ©2014 by Daniel J. Langton

All rights reserved. Printed in the United States of America. No part of this book may be used or reproduced in any manner whatsoever without written permission except in the case of brief quotations embodied in critical articles and reviews. For information contact:

1ST WORLD LIBRARY
PO Box 2211
Fairfield, Iowa 52556
www.1stworldpublishing.com

BLUE LIGHT PRESS
www.bluelightpress.com
Email: bluelightpress@aol.com

BOOK & COVER DESIGN
Melanie Gendron

COVER ART
Melanie Gendron

AUTHOR
Dan Langton
P.O. Box 170012
San Francisco, California, 94117
www.DanLangton.com

AUTHOR PHOTOGRAPH
E.E. Van Brunt

FIRST EDITION

Library of Congress Control Number: 2014901799

ISBN 9781595408662

ACKNOWLEDGEMENTS

I wish to acknowledge, with gratitude, the editors who have published most of these poems.

Aisling
Alchemy
Apostrophe
Approach
Atlantic Monthly
Blue Unicorn
California Quarterly
Carolina Quarterly
Colorado Quarterly
Coracle
Dakotah Territory
Dalhousie Review
Denver Quarterly
Furquier Poetry Journal
Freefall
Haight Ashbury Literary Journal
Harvard Advocate
Hospital Drive
Hotel Amerika
Iowa Review
Kayak
Kansas Quarterly
Light
The Literary Review
The Lyric
The Magazine
Margie
Measure
Michigan Quarterly Review
Mississippi Valley Review
The Nation
Natural Bridge
Nebraska Review
New Mexico Humanities Review
New Orphic Review
North American Review
North Dakota Quarterly
Paris Review
Ploughshares
Poem
Poetry
Poetry Northwest
Poetry Now
Queen's Quarterly
Raintown Review
Rattle
San Francisco Review
Sandy River Review
Santa Clara Review
Ship of Fools
Song
South Dakota Review
Southern Indiana Review
Sumac
Threepenny Review
Times Literary Supplement
Transfer
Vallum
Verse Daily
Well Tempered Sonnet
Wisconsin Review
Yale Penny Poems
Yemassee
Zzzyva

TABLE OF CONTENTS

New Year's Eve	1
Abraham and Isaac	2
A Flight Of Stairs	3
Now Playing	4
One Poem	5
Remembering Golden Bells	6
A Day On Earth	7
A Burnt Offering	8
My My	9
June Twentieth	10
Holding A Chunk Of The Moon	11
Sleep	12
Somewhere In Norway	13
Today	14
We Close Our Eyes When We Sleep	15
First Things	16
December	17
Bosnia	18
Approaching	19
With Laurels In His Hand . . .	20
Of Stars And Men	21
The Three Visits	24
The Marriage of Anne	28
The Indifferent Beak	36
The First Day Of Summer	40
Not The Thing Itself, But The Poetry Of The Thing	45
Sunday	47
Souvenirs	48
Rainy Day	49
Law And Order	50
If My Poems Had An Index	51

Dedication	52
In Chile Now, Cherries Are Dancing	53
Letter To A Poet Who Has Never Left Tibet	54
Kaleidoscope	55
It Isn't As If	57
On Spending A Week With A Very Beautiful, Very Young Girl	58
You Can Only Imagine	59
An Explanation To The Assistant Manager	60
This Year's Poem	61
The Old Woman Of Grosse Pointe	62
The Light By The Door	63
The Japanese Tea Garden	64
The Girl From Durango	66
P O P C O R N	67
Nightfall; Victoria Embankment	68
Learning French	69
If You Need Assistance	70
For A Woman Who Would Be Young Again	71
Flesh Wound	73
Fin	74
D N A	75
Saying Goodbye To Richard	76
Pantoum For Parker Mills	77
Pantoum For Kymrie Mills	79
A Sonnet For David	81
Soldiering	82
On Regaining My Sight	83
Bird Calls	84
Long Distance	85
One Time	86

October Eighth	87
Loss	88
Mark's Room	89
For A Sleepy Boy	90
With Her In An Urban Forest	91
On Taking My Wife To Dachau	92
Ballade For My Wife	93
Another Birthday	94
A Tuesday	95
A Thank-You Note	96
Married	97
A Poem About My Life	102
About the Author	105

NEW YEAR'S EVE

We know who's dying, not who's being born;
a boy who kills his mother as he's torn
from her will redeem the world, a dancer
we can tell from the dance, while an answer
we have always sought will come from a girl
in Afghanistan. A flag will unfurl.
Our Mozart will give us a threnody,
a hint of Lincoln, or of Kennedy.

Tonight so many look into the past,
the dusk, the useless rooms, the die they cast,
or see the time when they will be alone,
when they will put the stone upon the stone;
they should be buoyant, even as they mourn,
we know who's dying, not who's being born.

ABRAHAM AND ISAAC

My son, come here, the time has come
For me to tell you of the dread
I've felt since you became a man.
Lay down the sticks, I'll now reveal

How God, in all his wisdom, said,
'My son, come here. The time has come
To change your name and start your clan
And, even as in age you kneel,

So shall you have a fruitful bed.'
And with his very words began
My son. Come here, the time has come
To start the blaze. It was unreal,

I knew, to think the Lord's own bread
Was mine to keep, I felt he'd plan
A time when he would test my zeal.
My son, come here, the time has come.

A FLIGHT OF STAIRS

Each nail bought — weighed — hammered — sunk —
The wood clean — brown — settled — held —
Tufts torn — boards measured — beveled — cut —
A flight of stairs up (down) a hill —
Bottom to top — nothing at bottom — wind at the top —
Miles from the world — the land lorn —
Rot — grubs — puddles — splitting sides —
Gaps at the nails — soft to the touch — weak —
Forty years of here.   Then poet.   Poem.

NOW PLAYING

This is about you,
about who you are.
Every copy of this
is slightly different;
this one for you.
It is changing
as you read,
you are changing
as you read,
the words above
have changed.
Don't look,
you've changed,
there are others
waiting to change
as you read this
and change.

ONE POEM

I had been writing until night,
I had just turned to light the light
when I looked out. A tall raccoon
had her hands on my pane, the moon
was reading over her shoulder.
It's all right, I could have told her,
I mostly sit, I'm not feral,
just about the only peril
is that you'll slip and fall, or I'll
keep smiling at your crazy smile.
First you must think, and I must feel,
I'm here to offer you a deal,
I will let you attend my home
if you will grant me this one poem.

REMEMBERING GOLDEN BELLS (Po Chu-i)

Not a boy, but better than nothing —
Kisses when you are old and gray —
Three Summers alive, and now three Winters dead.

I remember the day she died —
She made strange noises in her mouth —
Still, at the end of life, learning to talk.

I dwelled in the time before she was born —
I reasoned away the needs of love —
Shaking from me the ropes of grief.

So it was until this morning
When I passed someone she had loved
And I left my mended heart in her unsuspecting hands.

A DAY ON EARTH

A few minutes after the last human dies
a bison will be born near a bridge.
She will walk the bridge to a town,
she will browse in houses and stores,
snuffling calm poems and frantic diaries,
grow more collected as she goes,
dozing at random, grazing near bears,
the sun will light on her shoulders
and burn for a while in silent clocks.

A BURNT OFFERING

Of course it didn't happen, if it did
that would have meant that men who look like me
would have had to kill those who looked like them
as dulled workers in a slaughterhouse work around
the harmless cattle. No one would, God forbid
we could even think of it, could begin to see,
in our bruised imaginations, pictures of men
shoveling baked children without making a sound.

We would not be the same, would have to own
what we, yes we, had done, would have to construe
what could be saved, it would be our duty,
we would have to acknowledge, to atone
to Billy Wilder; when told it wasn't true
he was said to ask, *"Vo ist meine Mutti?"*

MY MY

It was the first good day in a long time —
Even dealers took their kids for a walk —
And I put on the Mamas and the Papas —
Stood at the window seeing marvels —

Dogs looked giggly
And the prick next door waved —
And I found I was saying out loud,
"I must have done something good,
I must have done something real good."

This is a poem for the angel
Who was given the privilege
Of naming the color of grass
And who jumped up and down
Waving her hand and shouting
Green!   Green!   Green!
Oh!   Green!   Green!

JUNE TWENTIETH

I did not die in Spring again this year,
I woke this morning and the world was there,
I felt the house rising, carried by birds
toward the center of song, scattering books.

In the last dream before morning the birds
had instructed me, preached to my quiet;
happiness, they trilled, is a memory,
a memory of something called happiness

I live in an isosceles world, I am
reminded of what never happened;
were you my love I would lie and tell you
of the woman stepping from a billboard.

I can make rhyme reason, and now I'm free,
Summer in my flying house, the birds berserk
with possibilities. I did not die
again this year. I own twenty-seven doors.

HOLDING A CHUNK OF THE MOON

An excited scientist, lean as chalk,
coming to see us and speaking at night,
the waning moon a faint shade of copper,
pulling a curtain across its broad face.
The scientist smiled, she wanted to talk
of lift-off and touch-down, effortless flight.
I put up my hand, nothing could stop her,
she flourished a rock brought back from its place.

It was in Indiana, in late June,
the days as long as long can safely be,
the nights assigned to help me understand
how I would live, why I could let the moon
speak for my heart, so that this stone for me
was just like holding a dead lover's hand.

SLEEP

I wonder why they call it falling,
falling is scary and falling deep
scariest of all. I'd like to keep
that out of it, start by calling
it something else. Slipping, creeping,
rising if I like, a sort of leap
to remind me there is sleeping
after love, and love after sleep.

SOMEWHERE IN NORWAY

Somewhere in Norway a cat I killed
lies formless on a highway's lip.
Afraid, I kicked his tired body there,
to lie like matted seaweed
in a wave's retreat. I stared across
and saw the farm where wonder
would descend when evening came
and ritual's milk turned cold,
until a boy was sent, to find
the antique fur alive with grubs,
and so to learn a lesson
I had never meant to teach.

TODAY

It's morning, the silence of things growing
covers the dripping world as butterflies
are witness. I stand among the snails,
the most like me of all the living here,
and let the arduous fun of knowing
lead me past my hands, my nose, my eyes,
into the petals of roses, details
of stems, until I can hear the here
and now burst around me like a small sign
to a huge destination. Inside, my wife
is singing.

       Some grieve the road not taken,
or build a cell they do not leave, or pine
for warships, pins and prizes, a speckled life.
Not me. I have my dream when I awaken.

WE CLOSE OUR EYES WHEN WE SLEEP

There is no need. I could watch for wild things
with a secret part of my quiet brain.
My mouth can be open, my ears don't close,
but my eyes shut out whatever isn't me.
I envy the creatures with fins or wings.
Of course I know I can harbor a train
of thought, plan my children, write poems, wear clothes,
but there is that something I want to free.

My eyes always open, like the shark or snake,
I would know the sun's promise, the dark's side,
I would never be inside myself, a child
with dubious toys called dreams, never take
my time as though I had time, and never cried
in my vacant cells for the treacherous wild.

FIRST THINGS

Sometimes the days just won't move no matter
what you try. First things, you say in the Spring
as you plant the brown rows, but the first thing
you see is they just won't come. The batter
stands interminably in the fresh sun,
tapping his yellow bat on the white plate.
Ball one. Strike one. Ball two. Strike two. At this rate
we'll all be dead before the first home run.

One night you hear on the phone, "Old Critchly's dead,"
and now it seems to bluster when it rings
and the boys say   Sir   when you walk to town.
Tommy Critchly!   What, what was that he said   —
I feel so good I swear to God it stings   —
and you call to the moon,   Slow down,   slow down.

DECEMBER

As I stare back it seems
my failure was I sought
to name the gliding birds.
I should have had less sense. Dreams
may be the way we thought
before we had these words.
What could I do but say?
I should have tried to let
the heart within the heart
and let it find its way.
I own a real regret
the mind has taken part.

BOSNIA

The houses on her street now looked like toys
that long ago were set in a safe place
and then taken out too often by fierce boys
who longed to leave the world without a trace.
When I found her body on the corner
there were figures singing among the ruins,
but they hadn't gathered there to mourn her,
they were calling on their god with soulful tunes.

Too many shattered clocks to give me time.
To dust thou shalt return. Not even this.
A tired soldier covered her with lime,
No place to hold her, no place left to kiss.
And I?   I wanted, I knew inside my dread,
to be the one crying, not the one dead.

APPROACHING

What we have is shaped, layered, planned,
like the twig of a bending sprout
covered with earth so it can grow,
the buds predicted by the shoot
that we can see and understand,
that we can seldom do without,
that only we can ever know
in all its style, within the root.

Some want to feel just what it takes
and think that they can know a storm
by studying the random flakes
that cling to the pane to get warm.
It seems no matter how they've tried
they cannot get to be inside.

WITH LAURELS IN HIS HAND...

Once, just before an air raid on Toulon,
a spy was leaned against an orphaned wall.
Two men tied up his hands and shot him dead,
then carried him toward the hole they'd dug
because they knew he'd die. But clouds were loud
and strung with planes before the job was done,
the soldiers panicked and assumed the grave,
were just in time to meet a pouncing bomb
and fill the air with chunks of startled cells.
The dead spy's corpse lay warm and whole and firm,
the young face tanning in the hot French sun.

OF STARS AND MEN

Man is made of ordinary star-stuff.
                        —Harlow Shapley

aus wie ein Stern: denn da ist keine Stelle,
die dich nicht sieht.   Du must dein Leben ändern.
                        —Ranier Maria Rilke

At first there was no night, nor any day,
No wind, no calm, no solid land, no sea;
Nothing but chaos in an aimless sway.
This is the way it was, Infinity —
A null where nothing stirred to live or die,
Nor were there any signs to prophesy
A change would come. Then from some spark, some blow,
Some screaming wrench, a heat began to grow
Inside that mass, the black to turn to blue,
The blue to orange, the matted core to glow
With all the perfect flames that blaze in you.

The cover of the shape withdrew, a space of gray
Bold solid stuff fanned out as though just free
From bands. The chunks whizzed out in every way,
They spun in what might pass for jubilee
If jubilee were part of this most dry
And timeless state. Some pieces went awry
And crashed and broke, others began to slow

To take their places circling high or low
About their light. The earth, a hot thin stew,
Whipped into line, seething within its row
With all the perfect flames that blaze in you.

A crust began to form of livid clay,
The earth to take its wrinkled form, to be
Itself, to feel and then in course obey
The laws that weaved its web, laws that decree
With unbent force the bend of sand and sky.
Warm mist arose, fat clouds began to lie
In dripping mounds above the land, to grow
And swell until they burst, until their flow
Had filled the sea and every hidden slough
Where first that barely moving thing might show
With all the perfect flames that blaze in you.

The sea was all life's womb; in every bay
The stones grew warts of splitting cells, algae
Greened the tides, thrived on their own decay,
Turned on themselves, crazy, drunk on a spree,
Tossing new forms toward the surface sky
That held upon its head the sun's warm eye.
Then life took heart, grew lungs to leave that flow,
To live on soaring rocks and sunless snow.
It crawled, it ran, it slid, it even flew,
And linked the pulsing nations from below
With all the perfect flames that blaze in you.

Man was the king of earth, no limb would stay
His weaponed hand, each wish was a decree.
Yet now and then the hunter was the prey
Of night-born winds that waved the mind's high sea.
So men built walls and grouped themselves, to try
To calm their dreams. They shaped a compound lie
Instead, a lie that swore they could outgrow
All niggling fears. First they must overthrow
The balanced chain, and then they must subdue
The million kinds of things that subtly glow
With all the perfect flames that blaze in you.

Now it can end, this time the wreckers know
Just how to reap harvest that they sow.
But earth will live, and men will live here too,
With all the grace that courage can bestow,
With all the perfect flames that blaze in you.

THE THREE VISITS

It was the Spring, I think, perhaps in May;
My father's death has blurred so much of that —
Now don't take on, no common tears for him —
He was a man, I think the world well knows,
So much too good for petty daily rounds
That death was like the shucking of a husk.
At any rate, this vision that I saw,
If saw is what I mean, came first to me
In warmth and golden glow; I feel the grass
Between my childish toes this very day,
Can still recall the sense of human peace
That drained my mind of divers kinds of things
And left it at the mercy of just one.

I've heard it said that visions are but scraps —
No, don't do that, the pillow's fine as is —
Of something we would give our souls to have.
But tell me, why was I not deeply moved
On finding there, that day, upon that hill,
A floating face I'd recognize in Hell,
That I cannot recall the time of day,
The day of week, or even just what month,
That all it was to me was solid peace,
So that I didn't run, or scream, or drop my doll,
But stood and looked, as one would watch the sky
If one thought one was lost. I did not move,
But not from fright, or awe, or rapture's touch;
Just stood my ground, as quiet as a child.

I hated her, you see, as though from birth,
As kittens hate to drown, or trout to breathe.
But nothing I worked up could long endure,
For when it came to that, my hungry spleen
Fed just as much on ignorance as not.
Above all else, I wanted that to end,
And formed the questions I was sick to ask,
But she just gazed, as though I were a map
That led its owner to a secret lake,
And then turned off, without a sign to me:
But I went down the hill in love with two.

O my hard father! now that he is dead
He seems so much more real. He was a man
Who cried to language for a word his own,
A special word to sum his many parts,
Father, teacher, leader, champion friend,
Torn like a loser's flag with love's excess,
Cringing but once, when he would talk of her,
Of how she burst his heart to hear it pop
And mashed the pieces with the heel of hate.
I see now that poor man's dampened mouth
As he would tell how she had spat me out
And cursed me as I grabbed for living air
And then, as soon as she could rise and walk,
Of how she left the farm for good and all
And how she died, among the arms of men.
I see him now, and know him to be wrong,
And know he meant it in his breathing heart,
And bless him for his try to save a child
By keeping half the horror to himself.

The next was Summer, birds as thick as hopes,
And I was walking on that self-same hill.
I hadn't said a word of her to him,
The peace I found might shatter on his mind,
For he had loved her so her given name
Upon some other wife would make him weep
Until his face was pruned with Winter grief —
And so I kept my new-found love to heart
And hardly thought of her, if truth will out,
As one will hardly ever think of air
Except in cyclones, or the gibbet's snare.
So when I found her I was not surprised,
She was just there — a part of all of me —
And I stood still, and saw her eyes were blue —
So that the sky and pupil were all one —
That she was fair, no skin for this fierce place,
That she could smile to make the fingers thick
With thoughts of touching that unsolid face.
I stared at her until the sun slipped down
And left me black upon that scratchy hill,
It wasn't till I lay in bed alone
I realized she had talked, and I had heard.

To know she loved him was a thing so grand
My lips would sing at any dirty chore
As though I combed my hair. It was so grand,
You'll never know, the trinity I felt,
Or how my heart went more and more to him.
I see your face, but I am dying now,
To blazes with your maybe, half-way love —
No — now I knew he'd had a worthy wife
I saw how much much more he needed me,
For other men get used to falling down —
Excuse themselves, get used to getting up,
But he was bleak perfection's daily guest.

He never could abide a loosening hand
And when he slipped, no word could give him help,
Just love, a constant round of steady love,
For those who can not, dare not ever bear.

And then the last was just before he died,
And empty eyes, I learned from her, can cry.
I felt the tears, they blended there with mine,
And as we watched his pain-gripped eyes went soft
And all the weight of forty iron years
Came crashing in the hands of two he loved,
A woman twenty, dead these twenty years,
A girl of twenty, dead since that damned night.

And now you know the illness cleaved to me,
I live with nothing but an urge to die.
My heart is not for such as cannot know
That every day's a choking in the throat,
People like me should slink the fields alone
And feed on what we dreamed the world would be.

As to my corpse, go throw it on a hill.
I know you folks, you talk of crazy Mae,
Who put her father in the ground herself;
Then took to bed, and waits there now to die.
But you know nothing, girl, of what it means —
Don't hide your face, I've seen your puddly eyes,
You're not a beast who reels from too much brain,
You're one of them, proportions neatly right.
Just do your job — my corpse off all alone —
And leave my darlings in their cellar home —
At peace, at last, forever in embrace.

THE MARRIAGE OF ANNE

I

It started like this:
A plain of yellow and green,
          supporting Conestogas.
A mild dawn wind
          chased before the sun.
The first quick-waking rabbits
          skittering,
Wakened by hunger
          and a familiar cycle.

Smell of grass,
          possibly grass,
Smell of water on the air,
          and the firm smell of buffalo.
Smell of men and women.
          On the dawn wind
The smell of rain.

Children under the wagons waken
          and wander downhill,
Look to the East,
Look for the sun,
          Shivering.

In a crowded wagon
            a woman opens blue eyes,
                  stares at a blue pan,
at her new daughter,
at her sleeping husband,
            without belief.

A man rubs a greasy hand
            in a greasy beard,
                  squinting from habit,
Finally stands at the flap of his wagon
Splashing his piss on the greedy ground.

A young boy dreams of Tennessee,
Of swish of gown on under-gown,
Wakens with a heavy hand
And spreads his sleeping wife.

Thunder,
            but no lightning.

The first up,
The walkers before breakfast,
Nod as they walk
Crooked against the unsure ground,
Bobbing around the wagons.

A naked girl,
        ten,
swims in the river.
The man who fathered her watches
and cannot understand
     his anxiety.

            In the wagon nearest the river
                      Robert awakens,
        Shiver in his bones.

        A girl
                who was sure she'd be first
                awakens last,
Sits in the light of her lamp,
Takes off her shift,
Strokes her breasts downward,
            then upward,
Strokes her belly from the top
            to the bottom,
Slides her palms on her legs
            from the bottom
            to the top,
Then stands and nods
At the empty canvas walls
As the sun finally flakes
The first white rocks.

This is the day
        Of the marriage of Anne.

II

        The sun floats across the sky
                with becoming majesty,
        warming to its task
        until it can no longer be thought of
                      as kind.

The noon meal is grand.
        Children bolt and dance,
            dogs yip,
        women cluck.
        This is a wedding day!

        Rev. Gloucender shaves
            for the first time in a week,
Winks at a passing friend
    for the first time in six.
Mostly it's been burials.

Anne and her mother prepare,
The mother shy,
The child intent.
Brisk hands adorn
The offering.

Robert tugs at the silken shorts,
    fingers the new wool shirt,
Stares in the mirror,
Looking for signs.

The violin perks up
      as Trumlin jiggles,
practicing his piece.
Let us hear it, Trumlin!
and the violin,
like a high donkey,
laughs at them
and they, good hearts,
laugh back.

A pig has been killed for the wedding
And eight big deer line a spit,
Beer has been crocked in the wagons
And countless cakes are cooked.

The boy, a groom now,
              has a pull of whiskey,
The bride a sip of wine.

At three the games begin.
A fighting match,
          Champion of the train!
A broken tooth and a clear winner.
A foot race.
A swim, twice across the river.
A shooting exhibition by the guide,
Who misses the target each time.

The all day threatening rain
    still blusters,
    still grumbles,

>   but the earth is still dry,
>   and the dauntless sun
>   continues by.

The people move to the center fire,
Nudging and pushing to have a look.
The bride and groom stand cold apart
Until the reverend takes their hands:

Dear God, these your children
are marrying God knows where
in the nation of the Cheyenne
determined to live as man and wife
and deliver unto this sweet earth
the children of their fidelity.
I ask you man to man dear God
to bless this marriage as it stands,
to give them husky children
and a tough old age.

:and he married them.

III

Twist and dance
        She married me!
Twist and dance
She married me!
Twist and dance
        She married me!

And I'll still have her in the morning.

Fires against the moon.
Dancers against the moon.
Dancers against fires.
Music against dancers.
Legs!   Legs!   Legs!

I'll still be dancing on my honeymoon,
I'll still be dancing at the end of June.
Give me a kiss and dance me quicker,
I'm getting drunk on this whiskey liquor!

Robert is drunk,
His eyes are blurry.
Glad he's drunk
And scared he's drunk:
Swing me in a hurry!

Stop for a drink and a rest, boy!

I'll dance all day and I'll dance all night,
I'll dance and wrestle and spit and fight.
I'll dance with her and I'll dance with you,
And I'll up and die at ninety-two!

And I'll still have her in the morning.

IV

Walking toward the place prepared,
Hand in hand in the gone-moon darkness,
Relentless as fire against fresh wood.

In the forest the she-owl shivers,
The round worm searches earth,
The river goes its private way,
Blood in the arms of the land.

Hands to each other's heads in comfort,
Lying among the staring trees,
Bodies thick with the earth's soft dust.

Then the rain,
The total rain,
And they go gratefully
To the horseless wagon.

And this is the end
      of the day
Of the marriage of Anne.

THE INDIFFERENT BEAK

I

The corn was all but dead, its fruit dead black.
The season had not turned, the sun stayed high.
The scarecrow drooped on guard, his fragile back
ground white by daily heat, the caustic cry
of crows long still. Beneath the tainted sky
the people came each day to shade the corn,
to stand in silence, and in silence mourn.

At first the priests were still, at length they said
the fever laid on earth must surely mean
the constant scorn of gods had struck the dead
with grave offense, that they at last had seen
the need for flames to heighten and to clean,
the need for sin to pay the deathless price,
the need for sin to pay with sacrifice.

It never had been done before, the cries
of startled anger made the priests retreat.
They swore they meant no harm, concocted lies
to make their sour words appear as sweet
as lovers' vows. They buried their defeat,
returned to handing out the meager bread
and praying to the sick and nearly dead.

The shouts died down, and all was as before.
Or so it seemed, until the children died
like stalks of corn, and nearly every door
hung thick with mourning weeds, untied and tied
from time to time with more. And then they cried:
Defend us   and the priests replied: We can't direct
the gods, it's from the gods that you defect.

They still held back but then the common well
began to muddy, buckets to come up dry.
The oxen died in thirsty rows, the smell
of swollen death clogged up the air, the sky
was tough with grit, for dirt had learned to fly
when birds had stopped. One day the word was said,
the priests were called and told to go ahead.

II

They picked her out by lot that very day
and probed her with their sticks from neck to knee,
and then announced they felt it would not pay
to send such scrawny evidence to plea
their fear of gods, the gods would only see
how poor the gift. They must avoid that slight
by penning her to feed her day and night.

They shaped a cage and had her lie inside,
told all the tribe to glean that she might eat
the best that could be found. A few defied
the priests, refused to bend beneath the heat
and turn the girl from neighbor into meat.
The others grubbed, and learned an aching hate
for this thin charge that they must help inflate.

For her, her days of hunger were now done,
her body's wrinkles filled with shining fat.
She lay all day beneath the sunburned sun,
at times would sing old songs for those who sat
on evening guard. A tame and puffy cat,
she ate and slept at will, until the day
the priests came in a body for their prey.

They freed the girl, and had her shuck her clothes,
then brought her to a place among the trees.
She held her mind apart, she knew that those
who loved her most would want to see her please
the gods by bearing up until the seas
of blissful sleepy death could wash her heart,
and drown the sins in which she'd taken part.

They wrapped her in the robe of their first chief
and sprinkled her with corn as though a bride.
The priests, their painted cheeks awash with grief,
stood in a circle while their leader cried
for heaven to end the dying when she died.
He stroked her hair and sang of human guilt,
then led her to the altar they had built.

III

Two days later, fat on the northern wind,
the blobs of rain came scarring dusty corn,
and all the disbelievers knew they'd sinned.
The people danced, and all the infants born
in that great week, as fast as they were torn
from mother flesh, were given to the priests,
who raised them for the guarding of their beasts.

And after that, each time the rain would fail,
they'd choose a growing girl and she would die.
But there came days when this had no avail;
except for blood, the matted land stayed dry,
the priests would say they had to try and try,
until at last the girls would wait in turn,
but still the sun would burn and burn and burn.

At last they left to find a softer land
where work and prudent hope were not undone
by blackened gods who ruled with heavy hand.
They took along their priests, who'd sometimes won
a day or two of peace from constant sun.
They roamed the earth, and left in every plain
the secret way they'd found for making rain.

THE FIRST DAY OF SUMMER

I

The sound water makes as it turns
past the rock, far beneath the air;
the sound between eyes; the heartened sound
of heat rising from disheveled grass;
the sound of the harp, the soloist
gone. Wait now, quiet, watch for the sound,
touch it with ends of tongues, know it
as it makes itself known: be sure.

In a park two children sing in French
of a small Japanese, the song brings
sound reflections in each of us
who hears it, the sand in the park
now touches the sea, now a stone fort
In Aden, or a place not at all
this place, or time, where a couple
standing still means to be one day.

II

With the finger tips, quiet as air,
the tips of the tips, the fingerprints
different each from each, the real turn
as the skin turns, the air as quiet . . . .
the rock in the hand will not split,
the ground will not open, the eyelash

opening and closing on the cheek
will not grow ravenous teeth: trust.

A man and a woman, potters' wheels,
their hands turn the warm earthen debris
into watertight beauty, their toes
send the wheels back to where they came,
just barely feeling the wheels, their hands
in the neck of the wet dirt, hurting
as the sun mounts Italy,
on a day as long as any.

III

Things taste, but they did not have to;
there could be hard or soft, runny
or solid, smooth or with deep dents,
hunger wouldn't mind. But there they are;
better, as always, than we would have
thought to ask for. Leading our lives;
singing in place;   the text of the day:
There is more than enough: come: take.

An old man eats a pale tomato
until his knife touches the center
where the end has come. Fastidious,
patient, untroubled, he puts his knife
on the ground beside a girl making
ideograms in the dirt. The girl
takes the knife to cut the words deeper.
The old man reads: hill   stream   fruit   old man.

IV

The air settles like the soldier birds
carrying the swamp on their feet;
parts of parts of things that live there
drift down and away, the soft landings
quickening memory, starting
the dance along the roof and sides
of life, the stirrings of the surface,
the turning, the turning at the top.

Patchouli, sandalwood, lupine
and cloves, bergamot, lavender,
neroli and lemon, skin and thyme
and Portugal, attar of roses,
cassia and rosemary, roof-
tar and laurel, grass after rain,
kitchens of lovers, babies' rooms,
fennel and pepper, boisterous June.

V

There is a place we cannot see,
placid and silent, cold as itself,
not part of us, just black, just there.
Then there are fish far from sparkling tones,
who died and went to hell, deep into hell,
swimming at random, waiting for rain,
motionless eyes painted on their heads,
motionless dreams painted on their nights.

Near-dawn, near the water, Summer's day,
the snakes sliding home, the wet earth
turning downward as the sun beams;
excited by light, the birds' eyes
break the surface of the dark;   absorbed,
the plants turn their heads, their colors.
The world is simple and compound eyes,
the waves come and clear the sky of night.

VI

The feel of wood, words in the dark,
the small light of the radio, pale breath
on the mirror, evidence, proof —
standing in the meadow, the earth
coming toward me, pushing through me,
the cricket as true as the mountain,
the world, not a part of it, leaving
the thought: Shadows are not what they seem.

Why do I remember, alone,
that day, the same as most others,
that tree, enough like the others,
that place I can no longer name?
I will be standing in that meadow
when I'm dying, puzzled as ever
by the tree, the cricket, the ground,
the slight delicious chill at day's close.

NOT THE THING ITSELF, BUT THE POETRY OF THE THING

I

The poet is after the unadulterated emotion,
from there to learn one thing from another,
to learn, let's say, how pebbles can be meaningful.
To start to see a design.
To become a gardener of truth.

II

When I was eleven
I held my brother's hand.
We were shy and blurty
but, you know, it was all right,
it was not the thing itself,
though that was peacefully part of it.

Later he lived with a Japanese girl
who widened his room with flowers.
She believed he knew flowers
till she found he thought violets
came from oak trees.
I started to love her too
when she did not correct him.
That Summer they walked in the country
and she picked violets, casually;
laughed at him the way Japanese do,
letting go for a moment
of an invisible crutch.

When she died,
and dying strangled the child
looming in her body,
he came to me
and talked of holding my hand.
I'd forgotten,
and of course not forgotten,
deep in the passages of me.

We did not hold hands that night.
But because we did once,
in the crux of life,
the terrifying thing
assumed a shape and form
and could be dealt with.

III

If you see any pebbles, pick them up
and put them in your pocket,
and look at them when you feel smooth.
Then read the young words of old poets
who grabbed for the pointless stars.

SUNDAY

Sean had me put all the black shoes
in the same bag, he put the pen
she'd scrawled the note with in the box
with her pins and brooches, the note
went in the fire, the words she wrote
liquid again. I piled the socks
on the night stand, thinking of when
I said to her, you have to choose,
and she had chosen Sean. The drawers
were empty except for pages
torn from papers of that Fall,
Fashion and Style and Back-to-School.

Sean started crying. "They're all whores.
I gave her all the advantages.
I wish I'd never . . . . . screw them all."
It was his turn to play the fool
so I just filled the shopping cart
with sweaters, and her underwear.
Worn out, I read the browning words
of 1991, what was in,
what not to choose, from books to gin,
what you could and could not afford,
where to go, what to do, not where
to trust and give your rapid heart.

SOUVENIRS

They are kept in sliding drawers, in rows:
announcements, short letters, fading pictures,
newspapers, a stray piece of heavy string,
ring boxes, though now with nothing in them,
medals and trophies, as far as that goes,
even the curling brown notes for lectures
I've forgotten, nothing there that can sing,
nothing with life's clear and lively rhythm.

Why are they here? Waiting for me like games
played in short pants with girls in pleated skirts
when we had all day. And why, if it hurts,
do I keep looking, remembering names
now just names, when I want the world to rhyme?
I can feel the answer. The past has time.

RAINY DAY

The king of China died
and all the people cried —
they sat in their chairs
and they pulled out their hairs
and they sighed and sighed and sighed.

O Wang Wang, King Of Us,
we'll make a terrible fuss —
we'll shriek and call
and scream and bawl
and the meaner ones will cuss.

They sat in a group and sang
of the wonderful reign of Wang —
they drank all the booze
and they peed in their shoes
while the cowbells rang and rang.

A king like Wang can't spoil,
they covered him with oil —
they put him in a pot
with a lot of whatnot
and brought him to a boil.

We'll miss our bubbling king —
that's why we sit and sing —
but everything goes
as everyone knows:
so Hurray for the Emperor Wing!

LAW AND ORDER

You know, I've been thinking;
Right now, in my house, I've got
Marijuana, nudist magazines,
Steel-core pornography, an underage girl,
A stolen library book, a complete set
Of Will Durant fraudulently obtained,
A hypodermic needle   and two funny-looking spoons.
Good thing I'm white.

IF MY POEMS HAD AN INDEX

childish whispers   Manhattan trees
harbors love   moves closer   moves away
grades his teachers   saunters in the rain
mother   girls   aunts & sisters   nuns
seen in Paris   tries too hard to please
thoughts on his father   September   May
Girls in Their Summer Dresses pain
private   enemies   buddies   guns
marries & joyful   living out West
plays the outfield   plays at writing plays
those he treasured   Bobby   Evie   Mark
learning to swim   Dickens   passing the test
movies   Shakespeare   living out his days
book he left open   the gathering dark

DEDICATION

Here's a book for my favorite bookie,
full of guys and puns and cornered nooky,
catching just right the classic tone,
the silver phrase, the primal bone,
slinky tethers and working jaws,
leaps that would make old Meno pause,
romps in the son of a foggy knight,
a rhyming drunkard, a jiggered fight.
Lesbia's down, the times are drab,
she says she misses your line of gab.
Come on over and you can ball us.
Up Caesar's ass!   Your friend, Catullus.

IN CHILE NOW, CHERRIES ARE DANCING

When I read Neruda I don't want to read him anymore,
I get so I want to see girls and gnaw pomegranates.
I want to borrow what he owns:
his house, his mother, his mother's mother, aquamarine.

No one who believes in death is safe,
his poems use the air-conditioning ducts,
they are bunched on roses, hitch on butterflies,
they are the price of water.

It is easy to be happy when he reminds you,
easy to see governments fall past poems,
to hear what the earth and sea are saying

It is easy to stop reading
and leave the book in the sun to grow.

LETTER TO A POET WHO HAS NEVER LEFT TIBET

We live in a house made of trees, my wife,
My son, a dog and I, we have a life
As quiet as a bee's; I try to teach
The four things I have learned, knowing that each
Will find a place to lie. (I've put the four
In other poems.) Like you, I guess, I'm more
A poet than a lover or a friend,
Though I am friendly, and my loves don't end.

As to my country, it is much too strong
To go the way it's going very long,
Our old are books we do not read, our young
Are never singing, and they are never sung.
I think we take more than we'll ever give.
There is a tax on flowers where I live.

KALEIDOSCOPE

You started to turn, and thought better of it,
you started to turn, heart dense with love,
the music ballooning to the happy ending
You started to turn.   Or did you?
your shoulder toward me, toward me,
the fulcrum of my world, you started to turn,
the left foot and the left side going left,
the eyes to replace the hair as you turn.
Or did you hesitate at the door, at the door,
to straighten your shirt, adjust your smile,
ready yourself for kindness to the indifferent?

Or did you hesitate at all, even start to turn?
When I am happy, yes, happy, the bluegreen wall
is free of insects, the songs are only songs.
And you do not turn, are resolute and dim,
flipping the door, going to get the mail,
Monday's child, clean and right as those
who kill for a living, the trout's head, the lamb,
and I celebrate you, rejoice in your displeasure,
the lines of your clothes, the brisk disappearance,
unfettered, jaunty, crass, leaving me to find
I am not crazy, I have not been left.

So I turn the tube of the past, slap its side,
I like it that my life is glass,
pieces I can see to, pieces I can not,
pieces that stop me and let me go;
you started to turn, you came running back,

you stay or you do not, the toy
that is my speculation, my haul of mirrors,
can only sprinkle the past in patterns
I can live with for the time. Turning and looking
and seeing, East or night, I choose, I decide
I see you turning, or you do not turn.

IT ISN'T AS IF

we were lovers. One full kiss on the stairs
that led to your room did not lead to your room,
the look in your humdrum eyes when we met
in the open air the same over the years
each time, the staid hand if I should assume,
should step toward you, should pretend to forget

I will not even hear that you are dead,
you will not care to hear that I died first.
The leaves were red, and then the solid lake.
I can not read your poems, you won't read this.

Well why then, why, when something's thought or said
that you would like, do I feel the clenching thirst,
the tightening of the mind;   O for Christ's sake
take back that time, those parted lips, that kiss.

ON SPENDING A WEEK WITH A VERY BEAUTIFUL, VERY YOUNG GIRL

For one thing:
I can't live on Campbell's soup, Cutty Sark, party and pot
        Campbell's soup, Cutty Sark, party and pot
        Campbell's soup, Cutty Sark, party and pot
I need some sleep, I need some clothes; my feet are always
        cold,
            my ass is always cold, my teeth are always
            cold.
My mail is piling up, my newspapers are piling up,
        my piles are piling up!
    Let me just listen to the news on the radio. Just the
        ball scores.
    Let me read to you for a while. No, not
        Omar Khayyam.
            No, not "Never A Greater Need".
Look, this is the third time — no, the fourth time
    today,
        and I think I deserve a little praise.
    Christ, an Olympic medal.
Look, tomorrow we'll pack a picnic lunch and some
    wine and some, some
    martinis in the thermos and we'll go to the
    beach,

        O. K. ?

    Oh, God, please don't let it rain.

YOU CAN ONLY IMAGINE

I would meet her at the railed edge of the river,
we had one season, it is only Summer dresses,
no coats, no boots, Spring sweaters or fine Fall colors.
It doesn't matter, I can't see her clearly now,
only bits and flashes, her eyes coming toward me,
her trembling eyes, a doughnut in her lustrous hand.

I was in love, but never excited waiting there.
She was married, and that was new. I thought of Hell
as worth it. You must always think of Hell as worth it
or who would wait at the railed edge of a river,
or lift the Summer from her, that was all there was,
or take the careless, paltry kiss of late-for-home?

I thought I had known love, she thought that she had too,
and when I took the train we cried so much we yawned.
I then thought love was writing, letters from the war,
my fervor in the airs I took, the adjectives
I heaped, the tart original phrase that sentenced her
to loving me until the cows came trooping home.

I duly went back there when arms died down; they'd moved.
I found her waitress friend, she told me what I'd missed.
My dear had never learned to read, and he not much.
So he had stood beside his wife, and read the words
of lust and passion spent, because they were to her.
I saw his finger trace the page, a glimpse of love.

AN EXPLANATION TO THE ASSISTANT MANAGER

The bottle said Raw Wild Honey
and there she was, brown and round
and in my strengthening hands again,
the morning sea as gray as the sand
as we scooped love like found money
in waves, not making a Puget Sound.
And as I thought of now; and then;
it slipped away from my puffy hand.

THIS YEAR'S POEM

I live 3.7 miles from you now,
I checked it on the thing in the car.
I can't get it down. Too many changes.
Too many things the same. Bobby is dead,
and I turn away from the dog food shelves
as though my face were too close to a fire.
The days are all the same, I have to do them
on my fingers, if that were Wednesday
two days ago then the garbage
goes out today, tomorrow the Laundromat.
Drought makes me read some poets, rain
others. The faucet key is missing,
someone has taken the sneakers.

THE OLD WOMAN OF GROSSE POINTE

I am at the age where my lovers are dead
in columns. Wide eyes, the sudden splash of pink,
the picnics near the graves we didn't think
were really full, when all we did and said
just came about, and love was one more sport
between the married and the single men
with prizes for them all. Who could tell us then
Life's tender has a melancholy port.

And now they're dead, and I forget their names,
just bits of color, sounds, a vagrant touch;
at first I sobbed at wakes, I liked the way
it looked, but now I'm tired of those games
and even of pretending it is such a much.
Tonight my daughter said, You had your day.

THE LIGHT BY THE DOOR

I am astonished by love. You would think
by now I'd have it right, that I would know
that jumping surge for what it is, would feel
sardonic and a mite amused.   Christ, no,
my heart is a playground, a dancing trink-
et in the tunnel of love, a pumping meal
for all who hold it dear, its pink
for girls, its blue for lack of them.   It's real,
each time it's real, each blessed time the po-
et is forgot, the teacher done, the zeal
for order in a pile, the missing link
a thunder in the brain, as off I go.

THE JAPANESE TEA GARDEN

Look into the world of the woman
in the Japanese Tea Garden
and you will see . . .

The girl so young
she needn't wear a blouse,
looking out to where
the shore is rumor.

The next biggest doll
a pretty young woman
naked before a camera,
an essay in geometry.

And then the mother
sleeping on her side,
soppy nipple falling
like a tropical idea
into the energetic mouth.

The lover, reflection in her eyes,
putting on her shirt for her,
not buttoning it.

This is the woman
in the Japanese Tea Garden
at tea time
holding a mammogram,
a letter from the king.

The carp swim.
Aimlessly, we say,
but we are not carp.
The woman walks in figure-eights
along the man-made edges
of the fishes' world.

THE GIRL FROM DURANGO

On a burro,
       a breast almost free,
    she laughed and laughed.
White dress and teeth: brown legs and face:
black burro and eyes.

    Sounds in Spanish — such sounds in Spanish
 I tilted my sombrero, making her slow with my squint.
And she was saying: *"Perdiste tus zapatos!*
 Perdiste tus zapatos!"

She was so beautiful
    I decided never to see her again
   And I lowered my sombrero
     Until the bells of the burro had vanished
      delicately into heaven.

POPCORN

We have moved too much, traveled too much,
My head is a hive of old numbers,
JUniper seven something something seven something,
The stocking caught on the phone,
The desperate one by one of the lies.

GArfield something,   9 0 2 3.
KLondike 5, whazzit whazzit ten.
Your phone spelled D A N G E R S,
Your phone spelled K L A A X X I,
Your phone spelled love once,
Something something once.

NIGHTFALL; VICTORIA EMBANKMENT

She would walk where the walking women did,
stones like promises underneath her gown,
turning to the water as to a friend,
her distant eyes like rings with missing gems.

The river's surface is a paltry lid
that never stops the quick from going down
to where the cringing and the terror end,
from going down to where the body stems

and checks the flailing turmoil till it's rid
of breathing and of doubt, until it's wound
around the coated knickknacks that are penned
like chapters in the history of the Thames.

The water closes like the door to Hell,
less like a river than a wishing well.

LEARNING FRENCH

Everything has to have a name
and right now. Even the park's ducks
are *canes* leading *canetons*,
my job is now *plongeur*.   Table
is now table with a sex.   Same
is now different, the hens' clucks
don't have a word to cling upon,
my accent barely speakable.

After all that, then what of you?
Mastery was to be my prize
even if it cost the earth.   It
was for my *camarade de jeu* —
just now you searched me with your eyes.
Maintenant.   Now.   Now it's worth it.

IF YOU NEED ASSISTANCE

I've left your voice on the machine.
I guess it will startle a few,
make others giggle, start a trend,
confuse the ones who cared at all,

asking themselves what it could mean,
had I forgotten, if I knew,
tempted to write, tempted to send
around, never tempted to call.

I heard your new one that one time,
"Harold and me are on the town."
I went a month without a poem.
What would I write? How could I rhyme?

I mean to leave it there, no one
will know how often I call home.

FOR A WOMAN WHO WOULD BE YOUNG AGAIN

Last night we danced by a mirror
In the home of a casual friend
And you turned your head in terror
Saying, "Don't dance that way again.

I think of myself as graceful,
When dancing I'm pretty and thin,
And I find it too distasteful
To eye the odd folly within."

I had no heart to reassure
Nor to say the mirror lied,
Though to my mind you're young and pure,
And shine like a sensate bride.

So now these words, these words to say
What could not at the time be said,
These words to calm an Autumn day,
To speak for me in firmer stead.

Here is a glass that never lies,
The poem submitted to the page,
This one to say your soul, your eyes,
All that is ageless, will not age.

Yours is a soul so brashly grand
It lines the seasoned face with youth
So those who see may understand
True signs are not the same as truth.

FLESH WOUND

Your letter rumples the window seat,
pleated as carelessly as the dress
you wore to Paris in another time,
when today was all there was, we had no past
and didn't know the future tense. You asked
for nothing, not even a question, sublime
in yourself, the world a rueful mess
you hadn't caused, love a religious retreat.

Now you write: What can we do if the centers
aren't holding, the edges are as dead
as skin about to fall, the things that mattered
are broken, bruised, smashed and scattered?
I remember that woman, and what she said:
The healing begins as the bullet enters.

FIN

You came in twos, your eyes, your hands, your breasts,
you were movement;   quick, flashy, quirky, deft;
you were the first among us to die of AIDS.
One day the easy stopped, the grueling tests
began, the nights, the corridors.   You left
the way a European movie fades.

Once no one anywhere had seen a flick,
for us it was our time, how it began
in darkened rows, Liv Ullmann, von Sydow
(pronounced sea-dove, you called Liv 54).
You wanted to be Jeanne Moreau, learn each trick
of her trade, traipse in Paris with Gabin,
You were one of those who led me to love,
one of those who showed me what life is for.

D N A

We mail letters to our wives,
when they open them and read them
they swell as we did, holding
to the letter with their spirit.
The secret is safe with them,
as from us, even as the letter
is read the envelope stays put,
the letters of the alphabet
become a proper noun, the
covering discrete; life is a tongue
unheard and understood, it will go on
to find the sense and take its chance,
as the brute must, as we can choose,
knowing of the words that mix and match.

SAYING GOODBYE TO RICHARD

Not here. Some town with Las or Los
in front of it. He had cancer,
the kind you don't fight, you just know.
Tan went to white, strong went to frail.
the turbulent life to a loss
of anger, of thrashing, the answer
off somewhere, neither Yes nor No.
His odd voice, "Very like a . . . . . ."

and then he stopped. And now he's stopped.
The calls he made will not be made,
the sons and daughters grow alone,
The poems he gave me, hints he dropped,
lie before me, the games he played
are mine. Well, then? Condone. Atone.

PANTOUM FOR PARKER MILLS

The world is just as new as once it was
Whenever love's strong waves send forth a son,
Whatever else the birth of children does
It leads grown men to feel there's something won.

Whenever love's strong waves send forth a son
The dawn of breathing life impresses all,
It leads grown men to feel there's something won,
It melts for just a while the graying wall.

The dawn of breathing life impresses all
Who in their grace can still be moved by grace,
It melts for just a while the graying wall:
We stand for one sweet moment face to face.

Who in their grace can still be moved by grace
Will know this feeling, and will know just when
We stand, for one sweet moment, face to face.
I am as sure as Job that all grown men

Will know this feeling, and will know just when
To praise the child, and thus to praise the truth,
I am as sure as Job that all grown men
Rejoice and glory in the birth of youth.

To praise the child, and thus to praise the truth.
Parker, I wrote this poem because of you.
Rejoice and glory in the birth of youth,
It gives grown men a fresh and lovely view.

Parker, I wrote this poem because of you.
Whatever else the birth of children does
It gives grown men a fresh and lovely view,
The world is just as new as once it was.

PANTOUM FOR KYMRIE MILLS

And now you're gone the world does not make sense,
the endless comfort of the tides is lost,
the air we need for thinking is too dense,
a line we didn't even see is crossed.

The endless comfort of the tides is lost
and lost, the fingers of the hand are closed,
a line we didn't even see is crossed,
the mirror's cracked.   It is as if we dozed

and lost.   The fingers of the hand are closed
around our closing dreams, we understand
the mirror's cracked.   It is as though we dozed
while robbers search our minds.   And now we stand

around our closing dreams, we understand
that there was nothing we could hope to keep
while robbers searched our minds, and now we stand
the pain as best we can, and dream of sleep.

That there was nothing we could hope to keep
insults the heart, it makes it wrong to mold
the pain as best we can and dream of sleep,
to think a life was just a story told

insults the heart, it makes it wrong to mold
then to another kind of shape.   We fear
to think a life was just a story told
to let life make a point.   First you were here,

then to another kind of shape.   We fear
the air we need for thinking is too dense
to let life make a point.   First you were here
and now you're gone.   The world does not make sense.

A SONNET FOR DAVID

> "the moral virtues which,
> after all, are the visible
> beauties of philosophy."
> —Michele Barbi

Absorbing all but green, the leaf is green.
Its veiny wings seduce the speedy dyes
except for one, a specter of the band,
that lights on minds still borne by childish lies.
A paradox, they say, that leaf and land
become what they reject. What empty eyes
such burghers have! they cannot understand
clear signs; the word 'reflect' is what they mean.

Between the seeker and the sought there lies
a soup of facts that wise old fools had planned
would turn the mind to matters more routine.
It's never worked, a hand will own a hand
that shares the lesson of that full surprise,
that sum of showing faith, that leafy green.

SOLDIERING

A gun on either side of me, a pond
with blood and foam, shit and corpses in it;
among the lily's pads, empty boxes
of bullets, bandages and processed food;
a quiet made up of too much blatant sound,
grass and weeds smashed by up-to-the-minute
shards of metal riven to find the fox's
hole I dug to do some transient good.

It is morning in her bedroom, soon she'll
dress and wander to her coffee, safe as sun,
while I huddle beneath a canopy
of shells, not sea shells, not the bursting shells
of peas, just chunks of murder left undone.
War is mere death, love made a man of me.

ON REGAINING MY SIGHT

The effortless intricacies, the lines,
the exact form and color of a chair,
the designs, everywhere the crammed designs,
nothing is blank, nothing is merely there.

For some it may be the first sight of birds,
that's true, but I would leave that to the deaf
who get to hear, to others cat-soft thighs
when once more they can touch, or playful words
when they can talk again, or to the chef
his taste, they all are fine, they are not eyes.

To those who have not known the stubborn dark
that wrapped its shroud about the best of me,
close your eyes tight until they leave a mark.
Then you will say, when once you know,   I see.

BIRD CALLS

I meant to come at dawn, birds being what they are.
But men being what they are it is nine o'clock
And I get birds like myself; loud, confident,
Charming, unarmed, jumping from flower to flower,
Light on their feet, always on the make, the sweet
Song just for song's sake, the chest firm,
The eyes soft, naked as jays, wearing no man's band.

The birds call, and I call, and the damned things hop
And I stand, watching the hop, my poorly-ground axe
At my knees, swelling with bird calls, doomed
Where I stand, nothing to do but get older,
Hop slowed, belly round, dreams parallel parked,
Singing my late morning starving song
While the industrious birds sleep off their worm.

LONG   DISTANCE

They called to me
to tell me my father
          was dying.
The wind was from the East
as I glanced at the trees.
Thanks, thanks very much, I said,
and that kind soft man, his arms raised,
waved goodbye from the ship of his days.
Old hymns and a lost communion
turned me as I turned away —
I stood again in that cold church,
my father beside me,
the clustered nuns before us,
the wind at my satin back.
My hand is still
so much smaller than his.

ONE TIME

Jim is chasing me
      across a roof in Harlem
I float like a pigeon
      between two cotes
Jim stops where tar meets edge
      all hands and knees
I would never do that, he says.
And now he has.

OCTOBER EIGHTH

I noticed the leaves today, I have been sick
and losing touch, but there they surely were,
falling from crowded trees, playing at sur-
vival, trying to make my brain as thick
as their gatherings, their wrinkled ends, their May,
lying like truthful books the winners burn,
told in a language I will never learn.
My brother has been dead a year today.

I think of all the poems that use the Fall
to euphemize a death, but Jimmy died
this blazing time of year, and all the kinds
of metaphor won't reach the boy I call
and mourn and hunger for, the boy who tried
too well. They are just leaves. Life teaches, art reminds.

LOSS

Someone who loved me has died. A big part
of that small team I listen to and write,
who smile when they think of me, call me Dan,
remember me when young, lay out their heart
when we wander and talk, know what is rite,
now quiet and still, there is one less man.

I know I should think of him. I should try
to be with him, to know the doleful nights,
the shifting thoughts of what he had, the sights
he would like to see again, his last sigh.
But I am here alone. Inside my head
I have the time when he is here with me
and trembling in the darkness I can see,
as plain as day, that part of me is dead.

MARK'S ROOM

The air is cold, yet blankets smudge his floor
as though my son were some wandering Russian
who missed the feel of home. I close the door
behind me, wondering if I dare rush in
where he has bearded dread. I move with care,
the heavy weight of parents, I full well know,
can smash the frail as if it weren't there,
as though we couldn't reap what isn't so.

I line the child, and tamp his rising heat,
audit the breath that marks the turning world.
Nothing brooks change, my passion to be neat
is lost in thoughts of him. His mind lies curled
about his dreams, I cannot change at night
what may be scattered toys, and may be rite.

FOR A SLEEPY BOY

In the time when there were no ships
sunk at the bottom of the sea,
singers sang of the naked maids
who swam or sunned on the fledgling rocks,
promising all the sweetest trips
as far as the eye could see, could see,
a place where the living never fades
and they still have no rules or locks.

There were those who went, none too wise,
but they never came back to tell,
to tell, whatever they lost or found,
the singers had to shade their eyes,
to make up tales of heaven and hell
for the people left on the ground.

WITH HER IN AN URBAN FOREST

The dense insistence of crows,
conversations on a train
in China, the darkened trees
looking ready to take fright,
the din, as far as that goes,
as real on our skin as rain
or the skittish legs of bees
out for the first time at night.
Then it was still, and all those
branches burdened with the strain
of silence bowed like Chinese
on the train, in calm delight.
"Eve," (before the moment flew)
"they all stopped to look at you."

ON TAKING MY WIFE TO DACHAU

The gallows were really there, the long aisles
Really there; light Germans in huge beds
Awoke at six, scratching their chests, their eyes
Unfocussed, showered and came alive, killed
People reluctantly, a little sadly, thoroughly.
Missed you somehow, my life, my son's first armor.
O the roads are so good, like in California,
The parks are square. On the level ground
There is a memorial, an insistence.

BALLADE FOR MY WIFE

The lonely know the length of every day,
misjudge the length of every lonely night,
the lonely know how much they have to pay
to keep the lonely mind from taking flight
where all their fears and loneliness combine.
I know the lonely know, as well I might.
O Lord, fill up all hearts with love like mine.

I saw you first when childhood still could play
quick games across your face, it seemed so right
that you ignored your youth, a small bouquet
some helpless lover sent. I was polite,
I shook your hand, my mind helped me recite
the mannered words, I waited for a sign,
and when it came my dingy soul felt white.
O Lord, fill up all hearts with love like mine.

The years have turned their back, the settling clay
is ribbed with slower blood. But, Eve, in spite
of all the winds that tried to bring decay,
I feel, as deep as then, the fine delight
that we once found, and finding brought to light,
the force that makes our life a sunny shrine
that few can understand, and none can blight.
O Lord, fill up all hearts with love like mine.

Princes and poets, the dullards and the bright,
the least, the greatest, all of this design,
give them, in kind, this gift, this inner sight.
O Lord, fill up all hearts with love like mine.

ANOTHER BIRTHDAY

More wine than we are used to, the guests gone,
gaudy wrappings, paper plates, the coarse smell
of unfinished food, intricate perfume,
all of this with the sun still out, the day
as innocent as can be, the front lawn
the same, as far as anyone can tell,
and there we are, in our familiar room,
thinking for once of what we cannot say.

Come with me outside, before it gets dark.
I have to show you what I know will please,
something between the truthful and the true.
I want to walk in our part of the park
so you can see; the leaves on the old trees
are just as green as the leaves on the new.

A TUESDAY

I handed you the letter he had sent
and waited by the door. What was the worst
that can have happened? That is what I meant
to say, before you cried, before you burst
into tears, if you will; before your eyes,
each of them, at the same time, showed a film
with scenes of photos of daunting size
that loomed as chaos over treasured calm.

I took the garbage out and set the table,
thinking of how the storm is always there,
a letter and a minute from our schemes,
tears have learned when to be on guard, able
to come at once when needed, to clear the air
of complicated plans, of structured dreams.

A THANK-YOU NOTE

I had never written a poem, not one,
when I met you, not counting the Latin
translated for classes. I'd never known
the faint brush at dusk of silk or satin
nor handled in the light what I could own
was mine.

         I think of all the things I've done
or seen or heard because of you. The man
in Kilkenny who said, "My God, your wife's
a rare beauty," as we danced at the fair,
my shy brothers, looking a new way at me,
all this I've had, all this, just so I can
write this sonnet to say to you: my life's
the second weekend of a love affair
each blooming day, as far as the eye can see.

MARRIED

> we take an overcoat of lies, as though the weather
> were always bad in the world of sexuality.
> —S. Freud

> for she was the only girl they loved, as she is
> the queenly pearl you prize
> —James Joyce

I

I am in my own thoughts
and do not see you gradually
or start to see you, you are there,
like coming on a picture
in the gallery of the mind.

The picture this; a long slow dress,
a book, your face to the book,
the grass greening to the creek,
the sound of nothing.

I am twenty and the snows
have become the creek,
the stones and the pennies clear again.
I am going to marry you
and I am thinking
and you are not thinking.

II

Hawks don't name things. The full handsome lift
under the wings is enough, the eyesight
good enough, the claws sharp enough,
the country below a place, a place for food
that lives without names for things: the water,
the grass, the sun, the shadow on the sun.

In the fresh air, in Dillon's Glen, near Troy,
walking from you, wrapped in the glen's chatter,
I mistake a hawk for a peregrine falcon,
city man in the barely dawn, all that
Dillon's Glen holds new to me, country dark
as real as sleep.   Danny, do you love me?

And lighter still: the Cooper's hawk is light.
The air growls, the wings snap, then sail,
the new light and the old ground are edges
of one another, giving each other the chance
to be there, fitting and tight and causing
this bursting, this garden, I will not name.

III

If life were a week you'd be Sunday
I feel like the ravenous shark
who's just heard the lemmings' splash,
I want to write you a song
to quiet the flapping butterfly:

Our love is child's play,
first times are like old times,
I can count to two too.
You have turned on the sound
and I feel like a ramshackle goat,
you are rain so fine
I didn't notice you starting,
you gave me honey and slumber
and I shall learn you by heart.
toodle dee doodle de doo

IV

Lovers are hatters who know they will go mad;
it's true!   before the creation of the kiss
we all just stood around, waiting for this
or that, waiting for god know what, some fad
or fashion, some way of striking poses
like peacocks or rams or stuttering cocks;
or sniffing urine, like the pretty fox
or even   (you saw this coming)   rubbing noses.

And so we did, and so we all still do;
I won't write here of what we went and did
except to say it's easy to forbid
and hard to stop, and harder to undo.

V

In my dream you wake me from a dream
to tell me of your dream, you are a nun
looking at a picture of a girl on
a rock painting a picture of a green
and pleasant land. You stare over her shoulder
toward the cooling sun, so that it seems
your clouded mind must squint. Traditions are schemes,
you tell yourself, and I'm just getting older.

You slide across my chest, your skating hand
as full as errant sun. I can feel the words
better than the hand, the heartfelt breath
better than the words. I thought of both, Dan,
it was all so wrong, as wrong as dead birds,
but then I thought, love's quite an answer to death.

A POEM ABOUT MY LIFE

I would find the road, and then the house,
Trying to look neat. "Well, there you are;
Before we start let's have some food."
Blue water pot, red faces, and white arms.
"Pay for my time, the other things don't count,
Materials and such. I have a hand
That all can read. I'll show you if you want."

So we would talk of price, my city fingers
Moving round the air, more strong than tough,
Making it seem to be right there already.
"We need it soon. This very day."
I nod, to say I know, for he has sought me out,
It was the name he heard, he says,
When he went into town and asked.
We sip at coffee with the bargain struck.

They place a table near the well's green edge
And I line up my pens, the way I do.
The children come and watch me work,
Led by the boy who means to do it too.
I let them stay, and let them see it
As it comes along, and hold it up
And, since they're young, show them
With what care I joined the reason's edge
And how it fit, just snug and fine enough,
And how it seemed one thing when first you looked
But when you looked again it seemed another.

Finishing as the children fooled around,
The parents back and walking toward the well,
Ready to read, and time enough to see.
I'd hand it over, and I'd watch his eyes.

And then he'd read it out
And they would   ooooohh and   aaaaaahh,
And then he'd pass it round
And they would pick out best
And next to best and so, the boys all fine,
The girls as grave as teachers, waiting
To see it grow inside them
Or to be of no account.

They'd fall to quiet, looking one to one,
I'd stand up then to go, and we'd shake hands,
I'd start across the yard in yellow light.
Turning to fix the gate, and not too shy,
I'd call across the evening, "Tell your friends".

ABOUT THE AUTHOR

Daniel J. Langton was born in Paterson, New Jersey and raised in East Harlem with his brothers and sister. He is married to Eve and they have a son, Mark. They live in San Francisco, where he teaches English and Creative Writing at San Francisco State University. His poetry has appeared in such journals as the *Nation*, the *Paris Review*, the *Atlantic Monthly*, the *TLS*, the *Harvard Advocate* and the *Iowa Review*, and has been awarded the London Prize, the Devins Award, the Edgar Allan Poe Award and others. This is his seventh collection.

Daniel J. Langton was launched into a life of writing poetry by William Carlos Williams. As he tells the story, "When I was just starting out, I went to a reading by William Carlos Williams. Afterward I showed him a poem of mine, and he told me, *I don't care what you're doing, quit your job, and write nothing but poetry.* And that's what happened."

Printed in the United States of America